B.C. It's A
Funny World

Johnny Hart

D1386545

CORONET BOOKS
Hodder Fawcett, London

Coronet Edition 1976
Second impression 1978

Printed and bound in Great Britain for
Hodder Fawcett Ltd., Mill Road,
Dunton Green, Sevenoaks, Kent
(Editorial Office, 47 Bedford Square,
London, WC1 3DP)
by Hunt Barnard Printing Ltd.,
Aylesbury, Bucks.

ISBN 0 340 20762 0

3-16

10·14

11·7

11.15

PHOO

THE ONLY WAY YOU CAN SEE THIS MOVIE, IS IF I TAKE YOU.

THIS WAY, IF YOU HAVE ANY QUESTIONS, I'LL BE ON HAND TO ANSWER THEM.

11·26

... SO YOU SEE, POP,... HIS HANG-UP WITH THE CHICK, STEMMED FROM HIS MOTHER'S REJECTION OF THE PARAKEET, WHICH...

kent

11-28

12.1

12·12.

12·17·

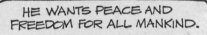

52-24

12·23

12·27

I HAVE COMPILED A BOOK OF ALL OF THE GOALS WE HAVE ACCOMPLISHED IN THE PAST TEN YEARS.

....BUT THESE ARE BLANK PAGES!...

12-30

WHAT GOOD IS A BOOK WITH BLANK PAGES?

...IT'S BETTER THAN NOTHING

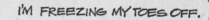

1·6

1·7

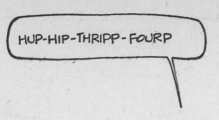

1:10

1·20

....THE SILENT MAJORITY STRIKES AGAIN.

hart

4

1-22

ZIP

CHUNK

1·27

1·28

1-29

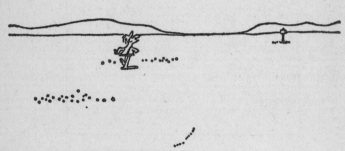

ZOT ZOT ZOT
ZOT ZOT ZOT
ZOT ZOT ZOT
ZOT ZOT ZOT
ZOT ZOT ZOT
ZOT ZOT ZOT
ZOT ZOT
ZOT ZOT ZOT

25

2.6

IT'S GOOD TO KNOW THAT ALL THE, ABSURDITY HASN'T GONE OUT OF THE COMICS.

hart

2.7

2·12

PLOP

OK, WHO'S THE WISE GUY?

2-18

2-20

2-23

2:29

hart

BONK

RESERVE

I HAVE SET ASIDE THIS PLACE SO THAT FUTURE GENERATIONS WILL HAVE A PLACE FOR 'WILD LIFE'.

3.2

TEE HEE

WHERE DO I SIGN UP?

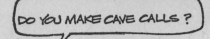

3·4

3.5

3.12

3·20

4-13

4.14

4·15

4-16

4·17

ZOT

Ptui

4·24

WHY DO I ALWAYS
GET THE SOLDIER
ANTS?

5.1

8

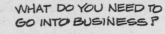

5.8

5·11

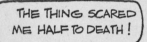

5.12

5.14

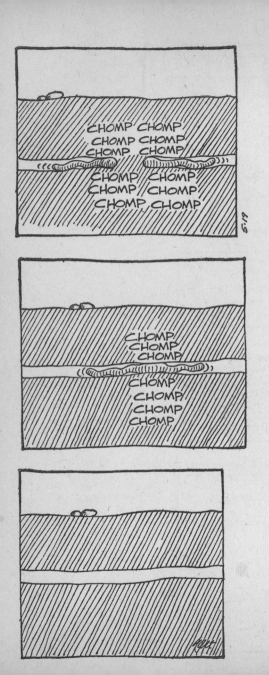

5·21

5:25

SIDE SPLITTING HUMOUR FROM CORONET BOOKS

JOHNNY HART

☐	18820 0	B.C. On The Rocks	50p
☐	19474 X	B.C. Right On	60p
☒	19873 7	B.C. Cave In	60p
☒	20653 5	B.C. One More Time	50p
☐	16477 8	Back to B.C.	50p
☐	16881 1	What's New B.C.	50p
☐	18780 8	B.C. Is Alive and Well	50p
☐	16880 3	B.C. Big Wheel	50p

JOHNNY HART & BRANT PARKER

☐	20529 6	Long Live the King	60p
☐	20776 0	Wizard Of Id Yield	50p
☐	18604 6	There's a Fly in My Swill	50p
☐	15818 2	The Wondrous Wizard of Id	50p
☐	16899 4	Remember the Golden Rule	50p
☐	16476 X	The Peasants are Revolting	50p

All these books are available at your local bookshop or newsagent, or can be ordered direct from the publisher. Just tick the titles you want and fill in the form below.

Prices and availability subject to change without notice.

CORONET BOOKS, P.O. Box 11, Falmouth, Cornwall.

Please send cheque or postal order, and allow the following for postage and packing:

U.K. – One book 22p plus 10p per copy for each additional book ordered, up to a maximum of 82p.

B.F.P.O. and **EIRE** – 22p for the first book plus 10p per copy for the next 6 books, thereafter 4p per book.

OTHER OVERSEAS CUSTOMERS – 30 for the first book and 10p per copy for each additional book.

Name ....

Address ....

....